A FLYING VISIT

T0382332

SIR SAMUEL HOARE

A FLYING VISIT

TO THE MIDDLE EAST

by

The Right Hon.
Sir SAMUEL HOARE, *Bart.*
C.M.G., M.P.
Secretary of State for Air

CAMBRIDGE
AT THE UNIVERSITY PRESS
1925

CAMBRIDGE
UNIVERSITY PRESS

University Printing House, Cambridge CB2 8BS, United Kingdom

Cambridge University Press is part of the University of Cambridge.

It furthers the University's mission by disseminating knowledge in the pursuit of
education, learning and research at the highest international levels of excellence.

www.cambridge.org
Information on this title: www.cambridge.org/9781107492868

© Cambridge University Press 1925

This publication is in copyright. Subject to statutory exception
and to the provisions of relevant collective licensing agreements,
no reproduction of any part may take place without the written
permission of Cambridge University Press.

First published 1925
First paperback edition 2015

A catalogue record for this publication is available from the British Library

ISBN 978-1-107-49286-8 Paperback

Cambridge University Press has no responsibility for the persistence or accuracy of
URLs for external or third-party internet websites referred to in this publication,
and does not guarantee that any content on such websites is, or will remain, accurate
or appropriate.

PREFACE

IN this little book I have brought together the material of certain lectures recently given in Chelsea and at Harrow School. As some of my hearers wished for a full account of what I said, I have collected together my notes and arranged them in chapters. It will be seen that they deal with the less official aspects of the journey. Questions of high policy, which I have purposely omitted, can be discussed in Parliament, and I will only say that the result of our journey should show itself in a substantial saving upon the Middle East Vote.

Thanks to Captain Euan Wallace, M.P., and others of my travelling companions, I have been able to illustrate the notes with some excellent photographs.

The author's royalties upon the sale of the book will go to the Royal Air Force Memorial Fund.

S. H.

July 1925

CONTENTS

ILLUSTRATIONS

A FLYING VISIT

THE OBJECT OF THE JOURNEY

IT was very necessary that someone in authority should see for himself the vast territories which the Peace Treaty had placed under our unwilling supervision in the Middle East. Political controversy had raged around them, millions of money had been spent in them and whilst many declared that they would always remain irreclaimable desert, others believed that they would become the greatest oil-field of the old world. Should we ever have undertaken the mandates? Should we ever have spent a single British life or a single British sovereign in maintaining order in Palestine, Trans-Jordania, and Iraq? Should we ever have accepted responsibility for the Zionist Declaration in Palestine or for the Hashimite régime at Baghdad and Amman? These questions, constantly convassed and never satisfac-

H.

torily answered, dealt chiefly with a
past over which few of us had any
influence. When I first became Secretary of State for Air in October 1922,
I found British power already estab-
lished in the Middle East. The question, with which the Governments of
Mr Bonar Law and Mr Baldwin were
then confronted, was not whether we
should ever have accepted the mandates
but how, having once accepted them, we
could with the least possible delay and
the greatest possible economy develope
the countries that had been entrusted
to our care. When I returned to the
Air Ministry in October 1924, I found
that, whilst some progress had been
made towards finding an answer to
this latter question, many problems
needed the personal visit of a Minister,
if they were to be understood at home
and settled quickly on the spot. Indeed,
the more closely I surveyed the outlook, the more strange it appeared
to me that, with the exception of the
visit which Lord Thomson made in

1924, no Minister of the Crown had seen the greater part of these new and distant lands.

For the Secretary of State for Air they were of peculiar significance, as they provided the only example in the world of countries defended and controlled from the air. At the Cairo Conference in 1921 Mr Winston Churchill, confronted with the huge expenditure of £27,000,000 a year upon fifty to sixty Imperial Army units in Iraq, had realized the peculiar fitness of the country for air operations, and had transferred the responsibility for defence from the War Office to the Air Ministry and from a G.O.C.[1] to an A.O.C.[2] For nearly three years, therefore, Iraq and Palestine have been under Air control and the Air Force has been given the opportunity of applying its own methods in its own way. The new Service needed such a chance, and it needed also the responsi-

[1] General Officer Commanding.
[2] Air Officer Commanding.

bility of undertaking a great and difficult command with its attendant duties.
So novel, indeed, was this Air Force
experiment and experience, that it became essential for any British Air Minister, who intended to study the use of
air in Empire defence, to see for himself the results of the Air Command in
the Middle East. Two years ago I had
made all my plans to visit Palestine
and Iraq during the Christmas recess.
The general election swept away, with
many bigger things, my own programme. When, however, I once again
became responsible, I resumed the project, and was happy to find that, just
as I desired to see at first hand the
defence activities for which I was responsible, so Mr Amery, the Secretary
of State for the Colonies, was anxious
to visit the countries for which the
Middle East Department of the Colonial
Office had been created. As the Prime
Minister and the Cabinet approved of
our project, we accordingly started upon
our joint expedition on 19 March 1925.

THE JOURNEY

I need say nothing of our journey by land and sea to Port Said except that the French authorities showed us their habitual courtesy, and Lord Inchcape, the Chairman of the P. & O., met us at Marseilles and took us over the *Razmak*, upon whose maiden voyage we were to journey to Port Said. Port Said we reached in strict accordance with the time table upon the early morning of 25 March. Air Commodore R. H. Clark-Hall and other officers, representing the Middle East Command of the Air Force, were there to meet us, together with the Egyptian Governor of the district and certain of his officials. The Directors of the Suez Canal Company had kindly placed at our disposal the quickest motor launch which I have ever seen, and we were soon rushing down the Canal to Ismailia at 40 miles an hour. From Ismailia we motored to our starting point, the Flying Training School of Abu Sueir, where our four machines were drawn up ready upon the aerodrome. The machines were twin-engined Vernons built by Vickers with 450 h.p. Napier "Lion" engines. They are normally used as troop or mail carriers and ambulances, and it may be remembered that from time to time I have given instances in the House of Commons of their value for taking small detachments of troops quickly from place to place and for evacuating sick and wounded from distant points to the central hospitals. Compared with Fighters they are slow. Their average speed is only about 70 miles an hour and, whilst they are excellent for the purposes for which they are required, they differ as much from a 9A or Bristol Fighter as a motor-bus differs from a taxi. Some of our party would, I feel sure, have preferred to make the journey in small open machines, but the long distances and the amount of luggage made it necessary for us to use these general omnibuses of the desert route. As soon as we had had an early luncheon at the mess, we got into our respective machines and started upon the first stage, to Amman, the chief and almost the only town of Trans-Jordania, situated on the table-land east of the Dead Sea.

We were a party of eight from Whitehall, Mr Amery taking with him Sir John Shuckburgh, the head of the Middle East Department, Captain Euan Wallace, M.P., his Parliamentary Secretary, and Mr J. A. P. Edgcumbe, his principal private secretary, whilst I had with me Group Captain C. S. Burnett, the Deputy Director of Air Operations and Intelligence at the Air Ministry, Mr C. Ll. Bullock, my principal private secretary, and Squadron Leader C. J. Mackay, who had recently completed a course at the Air Staff College. In addition to ourselves there were Group Captain K. G. Brooke, a senior staff officer from Air Head-quarters at Baghdad, to whom had been entrusted the arrangements of the journey, and one or two other Air Force officers. Mr Amery, Sir John Shuckburgh, Group Captain Brooke and I travelled in one machine, Captain Euan Wallace and the rest of the party were in the second and third, whilst our strictly limited amount of luggage was in the fourth. We left Abu Sueir at about 1.30 with a strongish wind against us. It was a beautiful afternoon with the sky even more blue and the desert even more yellow than usual. In a few minutes we were over the Suez Canal, a narrow ribbon that we could see stretched neatly out below us almost from end to end. The 28 dots that I counted were ships of all nations passing through it, one of them, a splendid five-masted sailing ship with Copenhagen and an eighteenth century date upon it, past which we had rushed in the Canal Company's motor boat. Then from the canal to the Dead Sea, continuous desert, at first with the Bay of Pelusium on our left and the line of Lord

Allenby's victorious march below us; next, branching to the eastward, the beginnings of the Dead Sea mountains. Formerly the route had continued along the coast as far as Ramleh and had then turned eastward over very dangerous flying country to Jericho. Now it is the practice to turn eastward about 100 miles earlier at Rafa and to cross the Dead Sea at the narrow neck that divides its northern and southern waters. It was this latter course that brought us to the desolate and savage mountains which had played so dramatic a part in the history of the world. Under a glowing afternoon sun the Dead Sea looked bluer than the Mediterranean and the mountains of every shade of brown and grey little more than indented hazards upon a golf links. As the contrary wind was strong, it was sunset when we reached Ziza, where we were to leave the Vernons and make the final stage of 30 miles to Amman in 9A's. The aerodrome at Amman is small for big machines and

the hour was already late for taking
any risks in the matter of landing,
whilst the upland plain of Ziza is as
good an aerodrome as anyone could
want. The change of machines did not
take more than a few minutes and I
could well have wished that we had
had more time to explore the interesting country in which we had landed.
For at the edge of the plain we could
see an ancient ruin that had been a
Persian hunting box of the sixth century, whilst the hills were dotted with
the ruins of Roman forts and the ter-
rain from which we rose had recently
been the scene of a remarkably successful air and armoured car action
against several thousands of Wahabi
marauders.

AMMAN

From Ziza to Amman it was only a
matter of a few minutes. The authorities, military and civil, were awaiting
us on the aerodrome, for at Amman
are stationed an Air Force Flight and

Colonel Cox, the Civil Commissioner for Trans-Jordania. As we were to dine with the Emir Abdullah, we had hastily to dress and to motor off to the hill-top upon which his new palace is situated. The Emir, it will be remembered, is one of the three brothers of the Hashimite family for whom, at a moment when ancient crowns were falling like autumn leaves, new thrones were created in the vicissitudes of the Peace Conference. Only a short time ago he lived with his court, winter and summer, in his ancestral tents. A visit to London had, however, somewhat surprisingly impressed him with the beauty of Buckingham Palace and induced him to build upon the mountains of Rabbath Ammon a building that, though considerably smaller in size, appeared to me to possess several of the depressing features of its prototype. It is reported in the neighbourhood that the Arabs when first they took up their abode under a roof, woke up with headaches every morning and that when it was suggested to them that it might be a good thing to open the windows, they answered with a question which appears to be conclusive: "What is the good of having windows if you open them?" Whilst I could not help wishing the Emir had remained faithful to his tents, nothing could have exceeded his kindness and hospitality. Outside the palace was a detachment of the Arab Legion, a picturesque irregular force, raised and commanded by Colonel Peake, one of the long line of remarkable Englishmen who have made careers in the Middle East; inside were the Emir in his Arab Caffya and robes, his minister Rikabi Pasha, formerly Governor of Baghdad under the Turkish régime, and several other of the notables. Around the dinner table were gathered the Emir's household, Arab servants, Nubian slaves and two or three good-looking Circassians from the colony which the Turks had settled in the neighbourhood some years ago. The dinner, which

was unfortunately more French than
Arab, gave me my first taste of Arab
coffee with its strong and bitter flavour
of Cardamom and my first experience
of Arab bagpipes with a power more
penetrating than the noise of two Napier
"Lion" engines in an aeroplane. Soon
after dinner the Emir retired, and we
went off to the house of Colonel Cox,
the British Resident, for a long discussion upon Trans-Jordan questions.
As it was only that morning that we had
landed in Egypt, we were all of us very
tired at the end of our long and varied
day. Mr Amery stayed the night with
Colonel Cox, I at the Air Force Headquarters, where I had a chance of
hearing much of the delights of the
climate and the excellence of the sport
in the surrounding districts. The servant who unpacked my bag I found to
be a Russian, one of those many wanderers from the army of Denikin, in
which he had won a commission.
Everywhere in the Near and Middle
East you come on this flotsam and

jetsam of the great wreck. Here at
Amman I had recalled to me many of the
incidents which I had seen in Russia.
In a few days' time I had once again
to pull out my rusty Russian in Baghdad; at Jerusalem, a week or two later,
it was once more in Russian that I
talked to the servant who looked after
me. These countries, strewn with the
wrecks of former civilizations and
covered with the remnants of their
populations, have in these later years
seen the arrival of many penniless
wanderers from an empire which our
fathers believed would soon enter them
as a conqueror.

FROM AMMAN TO BAGHDAD

Early the next morning we met upon
the aerodrome and again made our
change of machines at Ziza. The stage
of the previous day had been somewhat less than 300 miles and we had

taken three hours and fifty minutes.
Our next stage was to be much longer,
for from Amman to Baghdad it is 532
miles and the average time is about
seven hours. A journey of seven hours
in a shut machine, even though you
sit in a comfortable chair and can
normally read and write without in-
convenience, is a tiring business. The
noise of the propellers in the air, the
noise of the two great engines on each
side of you and the monotonous outlook of the wide distances and limit-
less desert combine to make you feel
deaf and tired, when, without a moment
for recovery, you are expected to leap
lightly from the machine and say a
few bright words to the guard of
honour and the local notables who
have come to meet you at the aerodrome. Our second day, therefore,
was exacting. The desert gave as little
variety of view, for the lava boulders
beneath us at the start soon gave place
to a sea of sand that was only to change
its colour when the sand became the

browner mud dust of Mesopotamia. From time to time a few black spots upon the boundless expanse showed us the goat-hair tents of the Bedouin; from time to time also we could note the dark streak of the furrow that the Air Force have ploughed with Fordson tractors, over 500 miles from end to end, to mark the desert route for the aeroplanes. At length, having for some time passed the frontier of Iraq, we could see upon our left a long green streak bordering the line of the Euphrates, and in a short time a clump of date-palms which marked Ramadi where we were to re-fuel. Ramadi, a station on the Euphrates 803 miles from Cairo and 63 from Baghdad, proved in every sense of the word an oasis for us, for it gave us half-an-hour to stretch our legs and to have tea with the hospitable Civil Commissioner in his cool and shady house. We had been in wireless communication with Baghdad the whole day and at Ramadi we were able to fix the time of our

arrival for 4.30. Our last stage took
about 40 minutes. Upon the right we
had stretching in the distance the
waters of Lake Habbaniya and below
us for a considerable distance the line
of the Euphrates with its fringe of
cultivation and its criss-cross irrigation
ditches. At 4.25 we were circling over
Baghdad with our first view of the
majestic Tigris and the city, which, at
least from the air and during the night,
looks not unworthy of the glories of
Haroun-al-Raschid. We landed at the
aerodrome of Hinaidi, the centre of
the great armed camp built outside
Baghdad by the army at the end of the
war. Upon it were gathered together
the representatives of all the public
activities of the city. Upon the civil
side there was Sir Henry Dobbs, the
High Commissioner, with the mem-
bers of his staff, there were the Ministers of the Iraq Government, there
was a crowd of officials, British and
Iraqi. Upon the military side there was
Air Vice Marshal Sir John Higgins and

his staff, the representatives of the Iraqi
Army, and Colonel Girdwood, the
Colonel Commandant of the four
Imperial infantry battalions—the sole
remnant of the many units of five years
ago.

Our first duty was to inspect the
guard of honour and the one British
regiment still kept in Iraq, and a very
smart detachment it was of that excellent regiment, the Bedfordshire and
Hertfordshire. Then, with another vol-
ley from the cameras around us, we
motored off to the British Residency.

BAGHDAD

From Hinaidi to Baghdad it is in
the dry weather a windy, hot, and dusty
drive of seven miles, in the wet weather
an almost impassable sea of mud. The
entrance to Baghdad is unattractive:
you come in by a new street which the
Turks cut ruthlessly through the city
for the passage of their artillery and
you cross the river by a new bridge of

boats that was built under the administration of General Maude. A new
building also is the British Residency,
for the readers of certain newspapers
and of the anti-waste debates of a few
years ago will remember the outcry
excited by the expenditure upon a house
for the British Commissioner. I cannot
say now whether there was justifica-
tion or not for the outcry, but I can
affirm that the Residency is a house in
every way fitted to be the Headquarters
of the British High Commissioner and
that under the wise and hospitable
management of Sir Henry and Lady
Dobbs it is as delightful a Government
residence as I have ever had the pleasure of visiting. We arrived at the best
moment for the garden. The week or
two's season of poppies and roses was
at its height. On the one side of the
house were the date-palms and a carpet
of poppies and roses beneath them, on
the other the abundant and rushing
waters of the Tigris. At the door we
found King Feisal's principal aide-de-

camp waiting to welcome us to Iraq
and a pelican, the successive friend of
Sir Percy Cox and Sir Henry Dobbs,
somewhat suspicious of the arrival of
the Whitehall tourists.

Our first stay in Baghdad was to be
a stay of four days. We had so arranged our programme as to make it
possible for us to begin numerous discussions with the Iraqi Government
and with civil and military authorities,
and then to make tours in the country
whilst our proposals were being further
considered at Baghdad. Before, however, beginning our official discussions,
we paid, as in duty and courtesy bound,
a formal visit to King Feisal. King
Feisal was living in his new palace, or
perhaps I should say the series of
villas which he has built for himself on
the outskirts of the city. Much to my
delight we made the journey by river
in the High Commissioner's launch,
for it is the river that is the impressive
feature of Baghdad and it is the river-
life, with its barges and its tub-like gufas,

SIR SAMUEL HOARE AND SIR HENRY DOBBS,
WITH THE PELICAN, BAGHDAD

H.M. KING FEISAL

which brings together the city's chief activities. Although the landing-stage was only a few minutes' walk from the King's Palace, we found a row of motors waiting for us and the principal court officials ready to escort us. The house into which we were shown appeared to me to consist of a few big ground-floor rooms, in one of which we found King Feisal and all his ministers, King Feisal himself a tall and handsome figure in his Arab dress and the ministers in fez and frac. It was then that the Colonial Secretary displayed the retentiveness of his memory by plunging into Turkish, which he had studied upon leaving Balliol. Our visit of ceremony ended, we returned to the Residency for the first session of our official discussion. Into these discussions I need not enter except to say that, whilst Mr Amery had the opportunity of discussing many civil problems connected with the development of the country, I, as the Minister responsible for the Air Com-

mand, was principally interested in the
urgent question of making the Iraqi
Army more efficient and by this means
of effecting a gradual reduction in
British expenditure upon the Imperial
troops. These discussions took many
days and raised certain difficult questions. Before, however, we left Iraq
we had come to what I hope will be a
sound working arrangement between
the Iraqi Government and ourselves.
Interspersed with these discussions
were constant interviews and inspections, interviews, for instance, with the
military and civil authorities and inspections at Hinaidi, the Headquarters
of the Air Force and the Imperial Forces,
and at the Training Depots of the Iraqi
Army. One evening at a dinner party
given by the High Commissioner to
the Iraqi Cabinet I had a long talk with
the venerable Sheikh ul Islam, the last
holder of the highest religious post
under the Khalifs, now a refugee from
the anti-christian republicanism of
Angora and the Minister of Pious

Foundations in the Government of King Feisal. I told him that in a day or two's time I proposed to fly over Erbil, his native city, and that the journey would take an hour or two from Mosul. He had made this journey many times, was his answer, and had spent more days than the hours we needed for it. An impressive and wise old man, filled with religious fervour for the great days of the Khalifate and with patriotic anxiety for the Kurdish nation from which he was sprung. A second afternoon we visited another leader of the religious world, the Naqib of Baghdad, the keeper of the Holy Sunni places and a staunch adherent of British influence in Iraq. It was the Naqib who declared Feisal King, and who upon many occasions has given a lead to the public opinion of Baghdad. We found him in his fine new palace overlooking the Tigris and surrounded by every sign of wealth and influence. A man of a different type next whom I sat one evening at dinner was Ja'far Pasha,

a well-known leader in the Arab Army
during the later period of the war.
Ja'far, a fine soldier and a very cheery
soul, was captured by us from the
Turks, with whom he was serving, and
imprisoned in the citadel at Cairo.
Being a man of great enterprise, he
determined to escape and let himself
down to the moat by means of knotted
blankets; as he was also a man of great
weight, the blankets gave way under the
strain, and he was eventually recap-
tured with a broken leg. The military
authorities, either from a want or super-
abundance of humour, for I could not
decide which of the two it might have
been, took no further action than to
send him in a bill of 15*s*. 7*d*. for two
torn army blankets.

KADHIMAIN

Upon another day, when our conferences were ended, we motored off
under the guidance of Miss Gertrude

Bell to Kadhimain, one of the three holy
Shia cities of Iraq. Miss Gertrude
Bell's name is so well known and
widely honoured from the Middle East
to London that it would be imper-
tinent for me to say anything either of
her remarkable position in Iraq or of
her unique knowledge both of its antiquities and its modern life. Miss Bell,
having already held high administra-
tive posts during the war, is now the
Honorary Director of antiquities and
the trusted adviser of the British authorities upon Arab questions. I was
indeed lucky to have her as my guide
in the curious and fanatical town which
until recently had resented the ap-
proach of all Christians. Motoring
from Baghdad we saw something of
the ancient site of the great city of
Mansur, reputed to have held two
million inhabitants, and, passing by the
scattered tombs which everywhere dot
the outskirts of Moslem towns, were
soon within sight of the golden domes
of the holy town. Of no historic

interest, for it was a Persian prince
who recently gilded them, these golden
domes are a bright and pleasant sight,
the more so as they surmount a mosque
of many-coloured tiles. As no infidel
is allowed to enter a Shia mosque, we
stood outside with the mayor, an old
friend of Miss Bell, looking into the
courtyard and finally mounted the
roof of a neighbouring house from
which we had a fine view of the building and of the innumerable pigeons
which somehow or other clung to the
dome. The mayor, not content with
showing us the sights of the town, took
us to tea with him in a house of many
galleries and courtyards. I had once
attended a function that was described
as a " ricchissimo te d' onore " at the
palace of a Roman cardinal and I well
remember the abundance of drinks
and dishes that are not usually met
with at 5 o'clock. But the cardinal's
" te d' onore " was as nothing compared with the " te d' onore " of the
mayor of Kadhimain. Sitting at a long

table I counted the dishes, and I found that they numbered 62, each of them containing some new kind of crystallized fruit. The mayor sat in a corner watching his guests, for it was Ramazan and he himself a Moslem strictly *pratiquant*.

Somewhere or other the Princess Zobeideh, the wife of Haroun-al-Raschid, is buried in this attractive town, whilst the possession of two of the bodies of the twelve Imams makes it rank second only to Najaf in the veneration of the Shias.

MOSUL

On 31 March we started upon our tour to Mosul and the north. From Baghdad to Mosul it is 220 miles and it took us three hours and a half. The Sheikh ul Islam had told me that under the Turks the mail took a fortnight for the journey. Striking north up the line of the Tigris, we were soon looking down upon what appeared to be a

great circular city, of hundreds of thousands of inhabitants, with a golden
dome in its midst. It was the ruins of
Samarra, the city which, stretching for
21 miles, was for seven generations the
capital of the Abbassid Khalifs. From
the air it still appeared to be a complete and inhabited town, for, from the
air, ruins, which are scarcely visible
upon the ground of the desert, retain
the appearance of streets and walls and
even houses. In a couple of hours we
were circling over a still more ancient
and historic site. In front of us were
the waters of the Tigris, even wider
and stronger than at Baghdad, flanked
on the further side by the straggling
whiteness of Mosul and beneath us a
long and undulating plateau that had
once been the great city of Nineveh.
At the south end of this plateau rose
the minarets of Nebi Yunus, a Moslem
shrine which, by a curious confusion
of religious traditions, is reputed to
contain the remains of the Prophet
Jonah, but is in reality the tomb of a

THE SECRETARIES OF STATE WITH NURI PASHA

AIR FORCE HEADQUARTERS, MOSUL

ASSYRIAN LEVIES

highly-esteemed Christian archbishop. When later in the day I roamed about the site, I was greatly impressed by the strength of the position and by the wide expanse which the city covered. Being no archæologist, I had no means of judging whether these miles of deserted plateau had still treasures to surrender such as not even Sir Henry Layard had discovered in his famous expedition.

Upon the aerodrome were the representatives of the various units, the Commanding Officers of the Air Force squadrons and the Armoured Car Company, the second in command of the Levies, about whom I shall say more in a subsequent chapter, Nuri Pasha, the Deputy Commander-in-Chief of the Iraq Army and the active and intelligent British Civil Commissioner, in whom I found a Chelsea constituent. Colonel Brown, formerly of the 14th Hussars, who, in the absence of the Colonel Commandant, was commanding the Levies, took me

off to his Headquarters, a great house
built around a courtyard of steel-grey
Mosul marble, arched and carved like
a Romanesque cloister. Rumour said
that a Turkish official, whose total
salary had not exceeded £100 a year,
had built this palace out of his savings.

The next two days were filled to
overflowing with engagements of every
kind. We inspected the Assyrian Levies
and visited the quarters where, in accordance with Assyrian practice, wives
and families live, and live most re-
spectably, in the ordinary barrack
buildings. We had a glimpse of the
training of certain units of the Iraq
Army and a march past of the garrison.
We had tea with the Iraqi officers in the
Club recently formed in the old Turkish barracks. Most interesting of all,
we held a kind of durbar that evening
in the Government building to which
the notables of Mosul and the surrounding district came in surprising
numbers. The great hall was filled to
overflowing with men of many lan-

guages and many costumes. In a group
in front of me in scarlet and purple sat
the Chaldean Patriarch, the Vicar Apos-
tolic from the Vatican and two or three
eastern bishops. In a room on my left
we found an old man with fiery grey
eyes and a long white beard; it was
the Chief of the Yezidis, the Devil
Worshippers, a sect of about 20,000,
who, though disowned by Christians
and Moslems alike, live a not disreput-
able life upon the principle that, as the
power of good will always behave well,
it is only necessary to propitiate the
power of evil. Their temple is at Sheikh
Adi in the neighbouring mountains
where, as I heard to my regret, the
breed of sacred peacocks had recently
become extinct. In another corner of
the great hall I found two Englishmen
with the indelible stamp of British
N.C.O. impressed upon them. They
had stayed on in the country after the
war and set up a dairy business in the
neighbourhood of the town. Jews and
Christians were as numerous as Arabs,

for Mosul is a city of many peoples,
languages, and nations. Bedouin sheikhs
had come in from the desert and every
official in the district, British and
native, was there to see the strange
sight of two British Secretaries of
State who had arrived by air in the
course of the Easter Parliamentary recess. To their delight the Colonial
Secretary addressed them in Arabic,
whilst my friend from Chelsea was
kind enough to translate for me the
English observations that I ventured
to make. Perhaps the most interesting
personality of the neighbourhood was
not present at this varied assembly,
for the Colonial Secretary and I had
already paid a visit to Lady Surma,
the Chieftainess of the Assyrian Nes-
torians. Lady Surma I had known for
years. I first had the pleasure of meet-
ing her when, at the time of the Peace
Conference, she came to plead the
cause of the remnant of the great
Assyrian nation. I remember well the
impression which this remarkable lady

THE CHIEF OF THE DEVIL
WORSHIPPERS

THE MUTESARRIF OF SULAIMANIYA

made upon all with whom she came in
contact. Even Lord Curzon, who was
by no means responsive to the ap-
proaches of the many suitors of the
Peace, was almost carried away by her
charm and ability. In perfect English
and with great feeling this remarkable
woman described to us a story of almost
unrelieved misfortune—how the last
remnant of this ancient race had fought
its way into British protection, how one
Patriarch had been murdered and how
another had died of disease, how finally
when the future looked more hopeful,
the Turks had seized their homes and
churches. I had brought her a letter from
her nephew, Ishai, the reigning Prince
and Patriarch, now called, in the style
of his predecessors, Mar Shimun. Mar
Shimun, the nephew of the last two
Patriarchs, is at present in England,
where he is being educated at St Au-
gustine's College, Canterbury. He holds
the distinction, unique in the history
of Patriarchs, of being an excellent
football player. We parted with Lady

Surma deeply impressed with the appeal for this remnant of a great race. As I left the Civil Commissioner's house, I noticed a little memorial in his garden set up by German pilots to two British flying officers who had died near Mosul.

HATRA

Amidst this rush of official engagements we stole an hour or two for a hurried flight to Hatra, the vast and almost unknown ruin of a Parthian city that lies far away in the inaccessible desert. Except for the fact that the Parthians inflicted upon Crassus one of the most crushing defeats ever sustained by the Roman Empire I knew little of their empire and its magnificence. In Iraq there are two splendid monuments of their power, the great arch at Ctesiphon and these ruins of Hatra which we visited from Mosul. Evidently Hatra had been one of the great cities of the East with its line of fortifications, its cisterns and the great palaces and temples, some of them still roofed, at its centre. Upon more than one occasion it withstood a protracted siege. The Emperor Septimius Severus felt certain that he could take it, but remembering the practice under which the loot of a city went to the commander if it should be surrendered, but to the troops if it were taken by assault, held back his men and set himself down to besiege it. His selfishness received the reward which it deserved, for he never took it. Of all the sites which I visited in Iraq there was none which I desired to investigate more than that of this unknown city of an almost equally unknown civilization. Hawks and falcons of every kind, including the beautiful white Persian falcon with black tips to its wings, had made their home in the ruins and I found a pair of hoopoes hopping from stone to stone in one of the great halls. It was curious to see together the falcons and the hoopoes, for is not Solomon reputed

3—2

to have given crests to the hoopoes and
to have left the vultures bald for the
shade which the former offered and the
latter refused him during a journey in
the desert? As I flew back, in a Bristol
Fighter, from Hatra, the Parthian city,
to Nineveh, the Assyrian capital, over
country which is totally uninhabited, I
could not have had a more conspicuous
illustration of the destruction wrought
by the Mongols in the thirteenth and
fourteenth centuries and by the dead
hand of the Turks since the days of
Hulagu and Tamerlane.

THE MOUNTAINS OF ROWANDUZ

On 2 April we left Mosul early in
the morning for a flight of two hours
and a half, first, round the mountains
and gorges of Rowanduz, and thence
by Erbil to Kirkuk. At Mosul it had
already been very cold, and as we neared
the snow-covered mountains flying at
a height of 7000 feet I would gladly

have worn two Sidcot flying suits instead of one. Rowanduz is at the head of the pass into Northern Persia. Its gorge is famous in the list of the sheerest gorges of the world and its situation has brought to it many expeditions and many clashes of armed men. The Russians—I know not whether it was a detachment of the army of that gallant old Cossack, General Baratoff—coming down from Persia, reached the pass during the war and a squadron of cavalry, seeing in front of them Turkish troops, and not realizing the gorge between them, charged and were lost every man and horse in the abyss. Since then Rowanduz has been the scene of a very successful operation carried out by Air Marshal Sir John Salmond two years ago. Unfortunately, as the landing ground was under snow, we could do no more than circle over this interesting point and thence make our way over the plain to Kirkuk. Half-way we passed over the sugar loaf town of

Erbil, the Arbela of Alexander the Great's victory, and earlier the high place of the worship of Astarte. Erbil stands round and high out of the desert, for town after town has been built upon the ruins of its predecessor. In the plain below I noticed the white tents of one of the Levy cavalry regiments.

KIRKUK

In less than an hour we were at Kirkuk, a place that is mainly Turcoman. Around the foot of the old town runs a long and picturesque bazaar, and the huge Turkish fort, in which I stayed, is the principal feature of the lower ground. Here I found two flights of the Air Force and a regiment of Kurdish irregular cavalry, commanded by Colonel Lawrence, V.C., an officer as well known in the British cavalry as in the show-ring of Olympia. Upon leaving the aerodrome we saw a parade of his regiment, and a fine sight it was

DH 9A OVER ROWANDUZ

KURDISH CAVALRY (COMMANDED BY COLONEL LAWRENCE, V.C.)
MARCH PAST THE SECRETARIES OF STATE

with the Kurds, one of the most war-
like looking races in the world, splen-
didly mounted and wearing a uniform
that was half Cossack and half Indian.
The boy scouts at Kirkuk had also
turned out to meet us, and in the afternoon there was the usual durbar of the
local notables. Later in the day Mr
Amery and I visited the Chaldean
Archbishop and drank with him many
cups of coffee and tea scented in our
honour with attar of roses. When we
afterwards visited his church, he and
his church council literally wept upon
our shoulders in their delight that two
British Ministers had visited the Christians of a town which in the past had
been notorious for its Christian pog-
roms.

THE FIERY FURNACE

Thanks to the knowledge and fore-
sight of our excellent British Civil
Commissioner we fitted into our programme a visit to the most ancient

oil-well in the world, and to the reputed fiery furnace of Shadrach, Meshach and Abed-nego. The oil-well is in the foot hills north of Mosul across a country which even the irresistible Ford found it almost impossible to traverse. For many centuries it had been worked with its primitive buckets by generation after generation of the same family. Are its leaking buckets to be the forerunners of the modern machinery and pipes that will exploit what some people believe to be the greatest oil-field in the world? Close at hand is the reputed fiery furnace of the Book of Daniel. Certainly it is a curious spectacle. Over a circle of 40 or 50 yards play innumerable flickering flames which, try as you will, you cannot extinguish. Whatever may be the natural explanation of this phenomenon, the tradition of the days of Daniel lingers in the neighbourhood and close to Kirkuk is the Prophet's reputed tomb. As we bumped back over the roadless country we passed Colonel Lawrence

with his pack of pure-bred salukis,
and his Kurdish whippers-in, out after
jackal upon the last day of the season.
It was a sight that needed the brush
of Alken—the Colonel with his splendid
seat, the Kurds as keen as any hunts-
men in Leicestershire, and the Arabs
and salukis adding the touch of a
Persian hunting panel to a background
of British sport.

DUST STORMS

We had intended to leave Kirkuk
upon the following day, but the head-
ache with which I woke made me
think that there was something wrong
with the weather. The feeling reminded
me of a really bad Italian scirocco, and
when I looked out of the window, of
the appearance of a London fog but of
a London fog made more devilish by
a gale of wind which very soon blew in
several of the windows. It was a dust-
storm that was raging, and it con-

tinued to rage for many hours. As any
idea of flying was out of the question,
we sat at home in the morning and,
when the storm had abated in the
evening, motored to see an Assyrian
villa which is being excavated by an
Italian professor. It was the season of
the year for dust-storms and in a few
days' time we were to meet another in
the south. The dust rises thousands of
feet into the air and many are the
Bedouin and cattle that die suffocated
by it. Fortunately for us the storm,
although it threatened, did not return
the following day and we were able to
fly without mishap a distance of 62
miles to Sulaimaniya.

SULAIMANIYA

Sulaimaniya is situated upon a table-
land in the Kurdish mountains and the
freshness of the green and the bright-
ness of its gardens might well have
been Swiss or North Italian. Outside

the town we found some cavalry of the
Iraq Army at drill, and inside, the
streets lined with rows of picturesque
Kurdish men, women and children,
who, contrary to the practice of the
East, gave vent to their feelings by
applauding the arrival of the two British
Ministers. For generations Sulaimaniya
has been the scene of almost continuous fighting; from time to time it
has been deserted and not even to-day
can one venture far from the walls for
fear of the marauding bands of Sheikh
Mahmoud, the local brigand; nor does
the perpetuity of blood-feuds help to
foster peaceful relations amongst the
inhabitants of the district. The principal
chieftains we saw at our durbar, for
the most part splendid-looking Kurds,
laughing and joking, ostentatiously
talking Persian rather than Turkish,
bearing themselves as descendants of
the great race of the Medes. One of
them with whom we talked was the heir
of the famous Lady Adela, the Kurdish
princess who for many years kept open

house at Halabja and governed her turbulent people with a firm hand. I wished that we could have stayed longer at this curious town and seen something of the Persian gardens, one of which a local magnate had made for himself during many years without any thought of spoiling it with a house. But the weather was uncertain, and we had still nearly 200 miles to fly to Baghdad. In these parts the middle of the day is always the worst time for flying, and we had a thoroughly bumpy journey before we reached Hinaidi in the middle of the afternoon.

Then began our second stay at Baghdad with a further series of conferences and a more detailed inspection of the Air and Army units at Hinaidi.

After four busy days we started in what appeared to be glorious weather for Basra and the south upon a flight of nearly 400 miles. Flying high we passed over two famous sites of ancient civilizations, the great arch of Ctesiphon, the last remnant of the Arsacid capital

of the Parthians, and the mound of
Babel, rising above what once had been
Babylon. Unfortunately it was not safe
to fly low, nor had we time to land.

DIWANIYA

As we proceeded, the clear morning
gave place to a thicker afternoon, and
we soon had a wireless message from
our pilot saying that owing to a dust-
storm we could not proceed further
and must land at Diwaniya on the
Euphrates. Accordingly, much to the
astonishment of the British Commissioner and the local population, our
three Vernons descended upon the emergency landing ground outside the town.
Within a few minutes the pilots and
mechanics had put up their wireless,
and were in touch with Basra, whence
they received a none too reassuring
weather report. It was clear that we
could go no further until the weather
improved and, whilst some of our

party remained with the machines and held an amateur concert for the entertainment of the local inhabitants, Mr Amery and I had luncheon with the Civil Commissioner and the Chief of the Police. It was near Diwaniya that the 1920 rising had broken out and we heard many stories of those critical days when, what with the heat, the distances and the desert the British infantry units found it almost impossible to operate against the elusive tribes of the Euphrates. At 4 o'clock it was thought safe to make a start, but when we had gone a few miles, a slight engine trouble took us back to Diwaniya. As it was now too late to reach Basra before dark, we wirelessed to Samawa to say that we would spend the night with a small Air Force detachment that was bivouacking in the desert. The sun was beginning to set when we reached the encampment, and the two British Secretaries of State descended from the skies upon the Air Force Flight encamped near the Basra railway and the river. Nothing could have exceeded the friendliness and hospitality of our reception. There were cocktails in a railway carriage, dinner in two series in a tent and much pleasant talk with keen young officers who were mapping and patrolling the desert.

As a heavy day had been arranged for us at Basra, we left the next morning about 6 and the wind being against us, took three hours for the 162 miles of the journey. Near Basra we were picked up by an escort from the squadron at Shaiba, and as we landed upon the aerodrome, it was curious to see a stork flying in almost exact formation with the machines. From the air Basra had appeared to be a draughts-board of black and white. The dried salt had everywhere made the desert white, whilst the blocks of date palms formed black squares in contrast.

BASRA

I found before me a long morning
of inspections. After Hinaidi Basra is
the principal military settlement of the
country. A big Air Force hospital,
our principal stores depot, an Indian
battalion, the river-craft for defence and
transport, the military prison and a
visit to H.M.S. *Lupin*, the sloop which
patrols the Persian Gulf, provided me
with a long programme under a blazing
sun. Hot as it was, the Captain of the
Lupin told me that he and his crew
come to Basra for a cold cure. Month
after month the sun beats down upon
the deck of the sloop as she cruises
about the Persian Gulf and, amongst
her other duties, now that the slave
trade has come to an end, gives medical
advice to the local sheikhs. I fear however that the pearl trade is too closely
cornered in the hands of the Bombay
and Paris merchants for pills for pearls
to become a useful and profitable

form of barter. When I had finished
my round and the day had become
cooler, I was glad to cross the great
Shatt-al-Arab, the confluence of the
Tigris and the Euphrates, and to play
an excellent game of lawn-tennis in the
beautiful garden of Colonel Ward, the
Controller of the Port.

ABADAN

For the next day there had been
arranged a long visit to the Anglo-
Persian oil-fields, but as I had a
Church Parade to attend I arranged to
join the party at luncheon at Abadan,
the Company's port. A day in Persia
I had imagined to be a mixture of
attar of roses and Omar Khayyam. The
Persia that I saw was an expanse of
unbroken desert, scorched by a fiery
sun, with an overpowering smell of oil
and a newly built port that would have
done credit to the Clyde. Row after
row of cylindrical tanks, fed by the
small single pipe that brings the oil

across the desert, were the chief features
of the view, whilst within the new
town of Abadan there was such an
array of enterprising Englishmen and
modern machinery as you might expect
to find in the most progressive districts
of industrial England. At the end of
a tiring but very interesting day we
motored back across the desert, seeing
at one point the encampment of a
scientist who was making geological
experiments for the Company and at
another the pleasant riverside town of
Mohammera, whose sheikh has so
recently been in trouble with the re-
doubtable Reza Khan. It was dark
when we passed the frontier post between Iraq and Iran, and by the time
we had crossed the Shatt-al-Arab and
returned to Group Headquarters I had
little time to dress for my next engage-
ment, a pleasant dinner and concert at
the Air Force Hospital.

UR OF THE CHALDEES

On 11 April we started back for
Baghdad, a distance which by the
route we had chosen was 315 miles.
Upon the way, however, we made two
halts, the first at Shaiba, the headquarters of the Air Force squadron, a
very well built and conveniently situated camp, the most popular part of
which appeared to be a swimming
bath; the second at a place of very
different character, for it was at Ur of
the Chaldees that we made our next
descent. All who have read the record
of Professor Woolley's work at Ur will
remember the remarkable character of
this great monument of a very ancient
past. The Assyrian ziggurat, built of
mud bricks, resembles a solid pyramid.
Tradition says that the Assyrian moun-
taineers built these mounds in the
desert to remind them of their native
mountains. Storey after storey was
painted in a different colour and

4–2

dedicated to a different deity, the winding passage along the outside finally leading up to the blue Temple of Heaven upon the summit. Could there have been a greater contrast in this country of many contrasts than the landing of British Ministers from an aeroplane upon the home of Abraham? If further contrast was needed, we found it in the arrival of a former Sergeant Major of the 7th Hussars who, mounted upon a good-looking arab, rode up with his native police troop and informed me that, although there were only two Englishmen in the neighbourhood, he was regularly hunting a pack of salukis with his sergeants as whippers-in and the Arab police as the field.

BACK TO BAGHDAD

For the third time we returned to Baghdad, finding to our satisfaction that much of the work upon which we had been engaged was nearing com-

THREE DESERT AEROPLANES

UR OF THE CHALDEES

ARAB POLICE

pletion. Of the many pleasant memories of this last stay two particularly impressed themselves on my memory. My old friend Sir Percy Loraine expressed a wish to see me for the purpose of discussing with me various Air questions, and the ubiquitous Junkers Company had offered to fly him to Baghdad. I gladly arranged for a British machine to meet him at the Persian frontier. Leaving Teheran in the early morning and changing machines at Khanikin, he arrived safely and easily at Baghdad in the middle of the morning, and, after a day's talk with Mr Amery and myself, returned in the same way the next day.

Then there was the dinner given by Sir Henry Dobbs to King Feisal, a dinner, like all Sir Henry Dobbs' dinners, of a most delightful kind but in this case specially marked by the hundreds of red rose heads with which the gardener had filled the fountain in the hall. How many hundreds there were I should not like to say, but there were not sufficient to make any gaps in the rose garden of the Residency.

On 14 April our visit to Baghdad and Iraq ended. Although our start was early, a gathering, greater than that which met us upon our arrival, saw us off from the aerodrome. Our good-byes were many and sincere, for during the three weeks of our stay we had made scores of friends. Particularly sorry were we to part from Sir Henry Dobbs and Air Vice-Marshal Sir John Higgins, the two men who, each in his own sphere, have worthily carried on the work of Sir Percy Cox and Air Marshal Sir John Salmond. It is not the object of these notes to scatter testimonials to British public servants, nor should I have the impertinence to praise men whose work is already known and appreciated by their fellows. If anyone doubts the excellence of the administration, military and civil, let him go to Iraq and compare the situation of to-day with the position of three or four years ago.

The band of one of the Indian units was playing as we mounted in the air simultaneously with a pair of sand-grouse disturbed by the noise of our engines.

For all that day the wind was heavily against us and the desert route, mono-tonous the first time, was not less monotonous the second. It was within five minutes of nine hours that the journey took us, with two short halts for re-fuelling, the first at Ramadi and the second at an emergency landing ground within an hour of our destina-tion. At this latter landing ground it was interesting to see the use made of one of the desert tanks in which petrol is stored under very heavy lock and key for the machines that require it. Indeed so strongly had the tank been reinforced against the raids of Arab looters that it was some little time before we could effect an entry and extract the tins which we required.

During the long hours of our flight there was little of fresh interest, and

I spent most of the day in writing up my notes. Once, however, when I looked out of the window I saw something that at once attracted my attention. For what seemed to be a considerable distance the desert was spotted with moving shapes. As we were not flying high, it was easy to make them out to be numbers of Bedouin, camels, sheep and goats. It might have been the Children of Israel moving forward into the Promised Land; it was, in fact, the great tribe of the Beni Sakr moving from one grazing ground to another, moving, not as many sheikhs now move with Ford motors for their tents and belongings, but as Abraham and the Patriarchs might have journeyed across this same desert. At Ziza we left our machines and motored along a road strewn with the ruins of Roman garrison life, to Amman, where once again Mr Amery lodged with the British Commissioner and I at the Air Force Headquarters.

TRANS-JORDANIA, PALESTINE
AND EGYPT

As the flight from Amman to Ramleh, the Air Headquarters in Palestine, is only 65 miles, I had the whole morning at Amman for inspecting the Air Force and for seeing something of the Roman ruins that abound in the neighbourhood. A splendid amphitheatre, in which a newly captured ostrich had found a home, a huge stone-encased cistern, still full of water, a line of forts, and the pavement of a great road all bear witness to the important place which Abdullah's capital once held in the Roman system of defence. The still finer remains of Jerasch I had no chance to see, for as in duty bound I was flying to Palestine, and could not, therefore, stop at them as Mr Amery and Colonel Cox stopped on their motor drive to Jerusalem. To me, at least, this wealth of Roman work came as a great surprise. I had heard of the wonders of Baalbek in Syria and of Petra in the territory through which I was flying, but I had never realized the extent or the interest of the other ruins which are scattered throughout the country. Professor Garstang, the well-known scholar in the service of the Palestine Government, is already at work upon them and I am glad to think that aviation has been able to help archæology and history by the air surveys which the Air Force has frequently provided.

In my former visit I had heard some talk of the sport to be had in the neighbourhood and I now had a chance of looking at the game book kept by the Air Force officers at Amman. In four days' shooting between November and February of last season they killed at Azrak, an oasis in the desert, no less than 2742 head, including 1103 green teal, 313 shoveller, 233 widgeon, 253 snipe, 215 mallard, 170 pin tail, 146 gadwall and 101 sheldrake. Truly, the life of the desert has some compensations to offer to the young officer who wants good sport at a small cost. I was not surprised to find that more than one of them was anxious to stay as long as possible in this sportsman's paradise.

The wind had got up when I started upon my flight to Ramleh and by the time that I had passed the northern shores of the Dead Sea we had to fly so high over the mountains that we were still above the clouds as we passed over Jerusalem. Ramleh, the Air Headquarters, is in the plain towards Jaffa and it was there that we landed for luncheon in the house which had been Lord Allenby's Headquarters and for the various inspections which I made before motoring to Jerusalem in the evening.

As I am not writing a Baedeker of the Middle East, I will not attempt to describe Jerusalem and the towns and villages of Palestine whose names and associations are the household words of Christendom. Let me only say that, thanks in great measure to the sympathy and imagination of Sir Ronald Storrs, the walls and the old town of Jerusalem are, quite apart from their Christian associations, more complete and unspoilt than anything that I have seen in Europe.

As certain recent incidents had deeply stirred the many Christian communities in Jerusalem, I was at some pains to attend the great services of the Orthodox Holy Week. From the time that I had spent a week's leave during the war at Moscow, and had scarcely left the Uspensky Cathedral a single minute of the night or day during the services of the Russian Holy Week, I had taken a peculiar interest in what are perhaps the most impressive and symbolic ceremonies that exist. I was, therefore, specially glad to find time amidst the conferences which we were holding upon various defence questions, to attend the Washing of the Feet by the Greek Patriarch on the morning of Holy Thursday in the courtyard of the Church of the Holy

Sepulchre, the same rite performed by the Armenian Patriarch in the afternoon and the Miracle of the Holy Fire on Holy Saturday. There is an ignorant habit of sneering at these great traditional services, at the credulity of the crowd, at the internecine jealousy of the Churches, at the want of reverence in the Christian Holy of Holies. I was actually advised not to attend the Miracle of the Holy Fire on the ground of its mediæval savagery. I went and, thanks to Sir Ronald Storrs, found a place in the Patriarchs' gallery from which I could look down upon the great crowd and almost see the interior of the Holy Sepulchre. Never have I surveyed so many human beings packed into so small a space. Some of them had taken up their stations days in advance, others had hired for themselves seats and boxes in the galleries, a baby had been born in the basilica that morning and another timed to arrive had unfortunately not appeared. Men, women and children were there of all the Churches of the East, Greeks and Russians, Armenians and Copts, Syrians and Abyssinians, for below me were the vivid black head and equally vivid white trousers of an Abyssinian prince who had brought Easter gifts from his Empress to the Abyssinian monastery in Jerusalem. Somehow or other a way was cut through this human mass, first for the rush of young men who in accordance with tradition sing songs against the infidel, next for the Greek Patriarch and the twelve banners of the Patriarchate and, lastly, for the processions of the Armenians, the Copts and the Syrians. When the Holy Fire broke out from the two sides of the Sepulchre, again a way was cut through the crowd for the runners who take it to Bethlehem. It seemed to me that considering the narrow space, the crowd of many eastern nationalities and these frequent entrances and exits, the people were both orderly and patient. In the whole building only one corner was empty, the gallery of the Cappuccini,

who are the Guardians of the Sepulchre. Many would say that this empty
corner was an outward sign of the
jealousies and rivalries which divide
Christendom. Whilst it is true that
every Christian should desire the re-
union of the Eastern and Western
Churches and the healing of all schism,
there is none the less the compensating
fact, so far as the Church of the Holy
Sepulchre is concerned, that the divided
sovereignty under which each part of
the Church is allocated to this or that
community has maintained a historical
status quo which would otherwise have
been destroyed. This same thought
struck me at Bethlehem, where in the
Church of the Nativity a window had
remained unwashed for years owing to
the divergent claims and rights of the
Greeks and Latins.

On the evening of Holy Saturday I
climbed to the roof of the Holy Sepulchre, where I found the Abyssinians
holding their Easter Eve vespers in a
tent. Sitting next to the Abyssinian

prince whom I had seen in the morning, I heard much complaint of the fact that, whilst his Church has an altar within the basilica, it cannot use it as the access is in the hands of another community. Within the tent were the Abyssinian monks, several in vestments of the most brilliant colours and in great mitres that looked like lamp-shades, chanting psalms to the accompaniment of drums and swaying backwards and forwards like the Dervishes whom many of us have seen in Constantinople. At half-time there was a procession three times round the roof, and I found myself dripping the wax of a big candle upon Bishop Gore, who was also assisting at this curious ceremony.

The English Cathedral, very Anglican and built after the manner of Magdalen, provided a contrast to these exotic services. I have sometimes wondered how it is that anything quite so English as Anglicanism makes its appeal to men and women of other races.

JERUSALEM FROM THE AIR

But even in Jerusalem, amidst the wealth of Greek and Latin tradition and display, it claims a chosen few of Arab adherents. One of them, an old and feeble man in Priest's orders, was left the last survivor of the Anglican community during the Turkish and German occupation—a timid old oriental, yet full of faith and a determination to uphold the honour of the great nation whose Church he had joined. As the war proceeded, British prisoners began to drift into Jerusalem and sixteen British officers died in captivity. Although the attitude of the Turks was daily becoming more threatening, this old Syrian sixteen times demanded a guard of honour from the German general for the Christian and white man who had died, and sixteen times marched through the streets of Jerusalem at the head of a funeral escort which, thanks to his bravery and insistence, did fitting honour to the dead of a great European country. The old man is dead, but I am glad to think that he lived to see Lord Allenby's entry and to hear the words of thanks which the General offered him for his courage and devotion.

These references to the services of Holy Week may make it appear that I was engaged upon a liturgical enquiry and not upon an official inspection. In point of fact I inspected every military unit in Palestine and had many valuable discussions with the High Commissioner, the A.O.C., Air Commodore Gerrard, and the military and civil authorities. There is in Palestine an Air Command, centred at Ramleh, responsible for the defence of both Trans-Jordania and Palestine, a British cavalry regiment and two kinds of gendarmerie over and above the local police of certain districts. As to the gendarmerie, there are the British gendarmes, a picked body of British, dismounted and in armoured cars, most of the men being veterans of the R.I.C. and the Irish Auxiliaries. When

I inspected them outside Jerusalem, I noticed not a few faces which I had last seen in Beggars Bush Barracks in Dublin, where, at the height of the trouble, I had visited the Auxiliaries and seen more medals and D.S.O.'s than I had ever seen before on a corresponding number of officers and men. The Palestine gendarmerie are locally recruited in the proportion of one-third Arab, one-third Christian and one-third Jew. Their uniform gives them a Cossack appearance and indeed one troop, recruited from the Circassians whom I had seen in Trans-Jordania, gave us a delightful display of Circassian games and dances after a luncheon held in our honour by the Inspector General of Police. One morning we had an interesting parade of this semi-military force on the small aerodrome of Kolundia, and an exhibition of co-operation in the form of picking up and dropping messages between aeroplanes and the gendarmes mounted upon horses and camels.

During these days Sir Herbert and Lady Samuel showed us every kindness at Government House, giving us one evening a dinner of 80 and an evening party of many hundreds, at which every section of the varied life of Palestine was represented. It was a mystery to me how the High Commissioner was able to work and entertain at Government House. For Government House is the huge hospice built by the German Emperor for the reception of German pilgrims. It is two or three miles out of Jerusalem and gave me the depressing feeling of St Pancras railway station doubled in size and built of yellow stone. But Sir Herbert Samuel is an administrator whose stride would be stopped by no such material obstacle as an incredibly inconvenient house. The hundreds of kilometres of good roads, the increasing number of telephone subscribers, the expansion of electric current are the monuments which a most distinguished ex-Cabinet Minister will leave upon the mountains and plains of Palestine.

As I had many Air Force inspections to make in Egypt I left Palestine a day before Mr Amery, flying from Ramleh first to Ismailia, where I looked at the site of the airship mooring mast, and next to Heliopolis, the aerodrome of Cairo. A strong wind blowing unexpectedly from the north helped us to do the 253 miles in two hours and fifty-five minutes, though certain of the party would have preferred a longer and less bumpy passage. My three days in Egypt, spent, thanks to the hospitality of Lord and Lady Allenby, at the Residency, were taken up with visits to Air Force units at Abbassia, Heliopolis and Aboukir, a long audience with King Fuad and talks with the High Commissioner and Air Vice-Marshal Sir Oliver Swann. One evening we were able to celebrate Lord Allenby's birthday at a dinner given to the principal British officials. No British general has a finer war record and few men have worked harder or longer in the service of their country. At a moment when, at the end of ten years' continuous responsibility in high commands, he has just retired from his post, it should be remembered that no man's prestige has stood higher in the Middle East than his and that no name will be longer remembered than the name of the British general who on foot entered the Holy City.

Upon the morning of 24 April, when the party and my luggage had left for Alexandria by train, I flew to Aboukir, a distance of 113 miles, to inspect the Air Force depot of the Middle East before joining our ship, the Italian Lloyd, *Vienna*. As we circled round Aboukir Air Vice-Marshal Swann, himself an old naval officer, explained to me the dispositions of the battle of the Nile. To-day Aboukir is composed chiefly of the Air Force depot and bathing huts for visitors from Alexandria. Near by is King Fuad's summer villa and a specially well-made road leading to and from Alexandria, over which we motored between an intermittent line of police which stretched most of the 15 miles. The police, I should say, were there to do honour to a British Minister rather than to protect him from the fate of Sir Lee Stack. For during my visit I had had many opportunities of hearing from varied and dependable sources of the great improvement that had been made in public security since the tragedy of last autumn.

ITALY

A two days' voyage in perfect weather and upon a most comfortable ship brought us on Sunday afternoon to Brindisi, where I was met by a squadron of Italian flying boats. It was at Signor Mussolini's invitation that we landed in Italy and broke our return journey for three days. During the war I had already had some relations with him at a time when his paper, the

Popolo d' Italia, even after the dark
days of Caporetto held aloft the flag
of the Allies, and when last I was in
office he had pressed me to visit Rome
and see something of the Italian Air
Force. As I had served in Italy for
nearly two years of the war and had
still many friends in the three services,
I was especially glad to be able to
accept this kind invitation. Although
our visit there was a short one, I none
the less had a chance of seeing something of the keenness and enterprise
of the Italian Air Service, a Service
which, it should be remembered, is
separate from the Army and Navy and
whose officers wear a uniform distinguished only with difficulty from our
own. It had been intended that we
should make a flight from the Ciampino aerodrome in one of the dirigibles,
and have a view of the combined
operations which the Army and the Air
Force were carrying out over Civita
Vecchia. Signor Mussolini, himself
his own Air Minister, and still limping

AERODROME, CIAMPINO

from a serious flying accident, was to accompany us. A gale of wind unfortunately made it unsafe to get the dirigible out of the hangar and I was prevented from making a second voyage in an Italian airship. My first voyage I had made during the war when I was asked to accompany upon his first flight a Lord Mayor of London who was visiting the Italian front and who, as I well remember, consumed more Mothersill in his drive to the aerodrome than I should have imagined the human frame capable of absorbing.

Visits to aerodromes, luncheons and dinners, interviews with the press, greetings of many old friends, made our three days in Rome pass all too quickly. They were sufficient, however, to confirm me in the view that I have always held that there is much community of interest and outlook between ourselves and the Italians and that particularly is this common feeling apparent in the development of British and Italian aviation.

And so ended our Easter holidays. We had heard many tongues, we had seen many peoples and we had visited places which would have taken the last generation months and perhaps years and would have needed many large volumes for the record of their travels. Our journey had been in no way a daring achievement. The time is past when a long distance flight can be regarded as a dangerous experience involving both risk and courage. Week after week some traveller, British or foreign, proves to the world the reliability of the aeroplane for flights to the uttermost ends of the earth. That British engines, British machines and British pilots are particularly reliable is a fact so well known as to need neither discussion nor testimonial. I do not believe that any member of our party, and there were several who had never flown before, ever felt the least nervousness during the 50 hours in which we flew 3500 miles. Indeed I am inclined to think that the danger of to-day is not the danger of exaggerating the risks of flying but of underrating them. Be this as it may, our journey went without a hitch, let alone without an accident. By means of flying we were able to carry out in all its details, and more than its details, a programme that without aeroplanes would have taken a year. We were given the chance to study difficult problems upon the spot and to talk, not through the deadening medium of minutes and despatches, but by the live current of conversation with the public servants, military and civil, who in the face of great difficulties have so well upheld the best traditions of British administration. It was the Air Force that made all this possible. I take off my hat to the officers who organized the tour, and it needs no small power of organization to carry a travelling troupe of Ministers and secretaries 3500 miles about the desert. I take off my hat to the pilots who in the ordinary routine of their daily training brought us without loss of time or nerves to our various destinations. I take off my hat to the mechanics without whose careful training and technical knowledge neither machine nor engine could work with such regularity. And I have to thank also my private secretary, Mr C. Ll. Bullock, whose imperturbable and infallible staff work inevitably earned him the name of Napoleon. Lastly, there are the men at home who in the factories and workshops built the machines and produced the engines. When I returned to London I was glad to go to the Napier works at Acton and say a word of congratulation to the 2000 men who produced the "Lion" engine which had driven us so well in the Vernons. No less gladly did I welcome the chance given me at a luncheon in honour of his new car to tell that great engineer, Mr Royce, of the excellence of the Rolls-Royces in the Bristol Fighters, that had carried us over the mountains north of Mosul.

THE AIR COMMAND AND THE DESERT ROUTE

Although I have finished the notes of my journey in the previous chapters, a postscript upon the Air Command in Iraq may be of interest to any who wish to know more of the interesting experiment that has been in progress for three years and a half.

It was on 1 October 1922 that the Air Force, under the able command of Air Marshal Sir John Salmond, took over from the Army the responsibility for the defence of Iraq. In 1920 there had been some 64 Army units and two Air Force squadrons in the country. Then came the rising and the garrison rose to 92 units and four squadrons. In terms of money the maintenance of these great forces cost as much as £38,500,000 a year, and even in the subsequent year, when after the rising the military units were reduced to 61 and the squadrons increased by one, the cost to the Imperial Exchequer was still over twenty millions.

This serious state of affairs brought about the Cairo Conference at which it was decided to make a spectacular reduction in the number of units and in the amount of expense and to carry out these economies by concentrating the defence upon the air rather than the ground. With a sudden fall the expenditure came down to £7,500,000, the Army units to 12 whilst the squadrons rose to eight. Since October 1922 further reductions have continuously been effected and when Mr Amery and I arrived in the country we found that the Army units were no more than one British battalion, three Indian battalions and one company of Sappers and Miners, whilst the number of squadrons remained at eight, with their ancillary Armoured Car Companies at three. In the course of five years the expenditure has thus been reduced from 38½ millions to less than four millions, and I have every hope that in a not far-distant future we shall be able to make still further economies of a substantial character.

When I quote these remarkable figures, I do not wish it for a moment to be thought that I am criticizing the Army expenditure of former years or suggesting that the Army is unfit to carry out the defence duties that are placed upon it. The Army can do much that the Air Force can never do, and there are many duties for which its organization and personnel are essential. But just as there are certain functions for which the Army is specially suited, so also there are functions, and the military control of Iraq is one, for which the Air Force is peculiarly adapted. In the 1920 rising it was found necessary to fill the country with a great army with all its attendant expenditure of men and money. Even so, the difficulties of the heat, the great distances and the lack of communications made the task of restoring order extremely difficult. In a country the greater part of whose surface is a continuous landing ground and where no counter from the Air is possible, eight

Air Force squadrons can, on the other hand, restore order and maintain peace with an efficiency and an economy of lives and money that are almost inconceivable.

This is not the place to describe in detail the system of the Air Command. I need only say that the greater number of the squadrons are kept in the camp at Hinaidi for instant use whereever they may be required and that within a few hours they can be concentrated on almost any point in the country. It has sometimes been asserted that this use of Air power is brutal and inhuman. As a matter of fact, compared with the long drawn-out operations of punitive expeditions it has been remarkably humane. In 99 cases out of 100 no bombs at all need be dropped upon a recalcitrant tribe or village. The arrival of an aeroplane within, it may be, a few minutes or a few hours of an act of crime or rebellion is sufficient to reestablish order and to impose respect for the central authority. In the hundredth case, where bombs are actually employed, the High Commissioner has himself to approve the action and preliminary warnings are dropped upon the threatened district. So far as British casualties are concerned, and I see no reason why, after the manner of certain critics, we should ignore the losses suffered by our own men in punitive expeditions, there was not a single death in action during the whole of 1924. So far as the natives are concerned, I am confident that any impartial investigation would show that their losses in human lives and in cattle have, since the time when Air Control began, been far less than they would have been in long drawn-out operations by columns of infantry and artillery.

But it is not only in the matter of maintaining law and order that the Air has been so successful in Iraq; the Air Command has also provided a wonderful training ground for the Air Force and many unique opportunities for applying Air methods. There is, for instance, the survey and mapping work upon which the squadrons are constantly engaged. Existing maps are so incorrect as in several instances to be from 50 to 100 miles wrong. Step by step an accurate survey from the air is being made of the whole country. Then there is the constant flying practice for the young pilots, often under conditions that resemble active service. No country and no Air Service has reached anything like the amount of flying hours flown by the Air Force pilots in Iraq. Whilst these advantages will instantly strike the attention of any observer there are others less obvious, but scarcely less valuable. It is good, for instance, that a new Service should have thrust upon it the responsibility of a great overseas command. Upon the shoulders of the A.O.C. and his officers in Iraq fall many responsibilities that carry with them varied experience in the management of men. Within the Air Force itself there is the

opportunity of working out a system
of close co-operation between the aeroplane and the armoured car. In Iraq
there are three Armoured Car Companies administered by the Air Command, and not a day passes without
proof of the special fitness of these
two mechanical inventions for con-
trolling a country of wide and flat
expanses. Outside the Air Force there
are the problems of co-operation with
the Iraq Army and the Iraq Levies.
The Iraq Army is a force of about
8000 men, officered hitherto by Arab
officers with King Feisal as Commander-in-Chief and Nuri Pasha as
Deputy Commander-in-Chief. The
Levies are locally recruited units with
British senior officers and native junior
officers. Of the seven Levy units four
are infantry battalions, three of them
being recruited from the Assyrian
refugees as frontier guards for the
Northern Frontier, and one of them
from the Marsh Arabs of the Euphrates,
whilst there are in addition two cavalry

regiments mainly composed of Kurds and one pack battery. During my visit I was very much impressed by the smart appearance and obvious keenness of these Levies. As for the Assyrians, it seemed to me that the one bright spot in their sad history showed itself in the three excellent infantry battalions into which most of their young men have voluntarily entered. Two or three efficient British officers, their tribal chiefs as under-officers, and still called by the Biblical name of Raab, the well-drilled men in khaki shorts and anzac hats with coloured plumes have created an atmosphere of self-respect and national unity that would otherwise have been finally extinguished by the wanderings and privations of the last ten years. Of the Kurdish cavalry I have already spoken in my description of our visit to Kirkuk. Here again is another example of the military effect of a few good British officers upon native troops. The Marsh Arabs I saw at Baghdad, where they provided the guard for the British Residency and had an excellent training depot.

These local forces, whether they be of the Iraq Army or of the Iraq Levies, are new and inexperienced, but there is no reason why in course of time they should not be capable of taking over many of the duties that are still carried out by the Imperial troops. Obviously it is to everyone's advantage, British and Iraqi alike, that they should become fully efficient as quickly as possible. I am glad to think that one of the objects of our journey was to expedite their development and I am glad also to think that it is one of the duties of the Air Command to assist, wherever it can, the formation of local forces strong enough in course of time to undertake the responsibility of their own country's defence.

Lastly, there is the Air Command's responsibility for the desert route. Once a fortnight two Vernons carry the mail between Egypt and Baghdad, a distance of 866 miles. It was at the

Cairo Conference that the decision was taken to open this route as a link in the chain of communications between Europe and India, as a line of rapid reinforcement between Egypt and Palestine and Iraq, as a means of rapid communication for Service purposes and last but not least as a form of training in long distance flying. Survey parties on Crossley and Rolls-Royce tenders from Cairo and Baghdad constructed the track and to make it as conspicuous as possible a Fordson tractor was used for ploughing the longest furrow in the world as a line for the aeroplanes to follow. In the course of a year a series of landing grounds were prepared at average intervals of 20 miles apart, each of them marked with a letter or number for the purpose of identification and each of them, so far as upkeep and salvage are concerned, under the responsibility of the Air Command either in Cairo or Baghdad. For more than three years the track has been kept open, and machines have been running with a regularity and reliability which every year has increased. It was over this track that Mr Amery and I made our journey, and it is over this track that many officials, military and civil, have been able to complete a journey in one or two days that would by land and sea have taken them a fortnight. To-day the air route has a companion in the motor route between Syria and Baghdad started by certain enterprising British subjects. I say "companion" rather than "rival," for I see no reason why there should not be in the future more than enough passengers and mails for both aeroplanes and motors to carry. Whatever developments the future may bring in improved means of communication, it can confidently be said that the desert route has fully justified the expectations of the officers who started it. Indeed so successful has it proved that immediately after our return the Government accepted my recommendation that the military mail should be developed into a civilian flying service between Egypt and Iraq and Iraq and India. That this development has now become practicable is due to the splendid pioneer work of the Air Force, which during the last three years has not only united the Middle East with an aerial chain, but has also tested over a long section of the journey the possibilities of a British civilian route to India. But here I am touching upon a question which, whilst it constantly occupied my mind during our tour, would carry me further than the limits of these notes. Let me, therefore, end them in the hope that though disjointed and incomplete—for most of them were written in an Air Force notebook during my flights—they are nevertheless sufficient to arouse interest, not only in a very remarkable part of the world, but also in a little-known sphere of British influence where Service and Civilian alike are carrying out a very fine work of British administration.

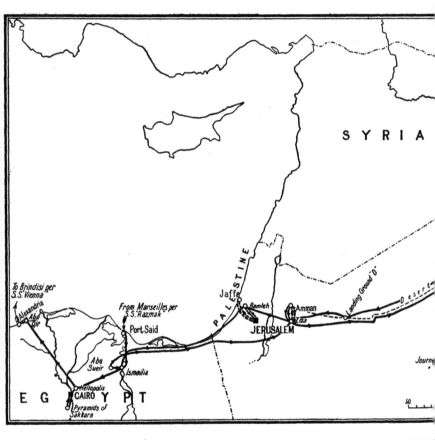

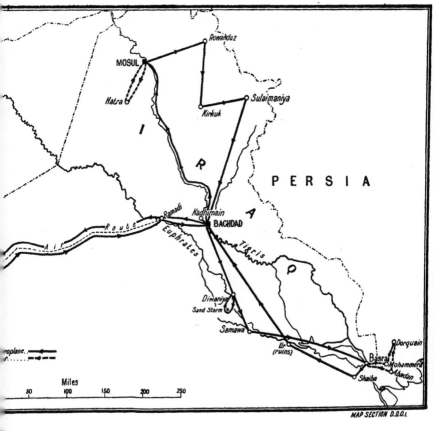

Rowanduz

MOSUL

Hatra

I

R

Kirkuk

Sulaimaniya

PERSIA

Ramadi

Route

Al

Euphrates

Kadhimain
BAGHDAD

A

Tigris

P

Diwaniya
Sand Storm

Samawa

Ur
(ruins)

Dorquain
Basra
Mohammera
Abadan
Shaiba

roplane.
n.

Miles
50   100   150   200   250

MAP SECTION D.O.O.I.

THE ROUTE

For EU product safety concerns, contact us at Calle de José Abascal, 56–1°, 28003 Madrid, Spain or eugpsr@cambridge.org.

www.ingramcontent.com/pod-product-compliance
Ingram Content Group UK Ltd.
Pitfield, Milton Keynes, MK11 3LW, UK
UKHW020312140625
459647UK00018B/1841